# Guess What

CHERRY
LAKE
Publishing

Published in the United States of America by
**Cherry Lake Publishing**
Ann Arbor, Michigan
www.cherrylakepublishing.com

Content Adviser: Susan Heinrichs Gray
Reading Adviser: Marla Conn MS, Ed., Literacy specialist, Read-Ability, Inc.
Book Designer: Felicia Macheske

Photo Credits: © Eric Isselee/Shutterstock.com, cover, 3, back cover; © andamanec/Shutterstock.com, 1, 4; © Edwin Butter/ Shutterstock.com, 7; © Kjersti Joergensen/Shutterstock.com, 8; © jeep2499/Shutterstock.com, 11; © Romas_Photo/Shutterstock. com, 12; © GUDKOV ANDREY/Shutterstock.com, 15; © Robert Lessmann/Shutterstock.com, 17; © Shanti Hesse/Shutterstock. com, 18; © leolintang/Shutterstock.com, 21; © Andrey_Kuzmin/Shutterstock.com, back cover

Library of Congress Cataloging-in-Publication Data

Names: Macheske, Felicia, author.
Title: Swinging smarties : orangutan / Felicia Macheske.
Other titles: Orangutan | Guess what (Cherry Lake Publishing)
Description: Ann Arbor, MI : Cherry Lake Publishing, [2017] | Series: Guess what | Audience: K to grade 3.
Identifiers: LCCN 2016029431| ISBN 9781634721714 (hardcover) |
 ISBN 9781634723039 (pbk.) | ISBN 9781634722377 (pdf) | ISBN 9781634723695 (ebook)
Subjects: LCSH: Orangutans—Juvenile literature. | Children's questions and answers.
Classification: LCC QL737.P94 M33 2017 | DDC 599.88/3—dc23
LC record available at https://lccn.loc.gov/2016029431

Cherry Lake Publishing would like to acknowledge the work of The Partnership for 21st Century Skills.
Please visit *www.p21.org* for more information.

Printed in the United States of America
Corporate Graphics

# Table of Contents

# I can see very well.

# I have long, shaggy hair.

My long arms make it easy to hang out in trees.

# I use my lips to touch and feel things.

I love to
eat fruit.
Sweet!

I can pick things up with my hands and feet.

# I live in warm tropical forests.

# I like to play.

**Do you know what I am?**

# I'm an Orangutan!

# About Orangutans

1. Orangutans have hands with a thumb like ours. They also have a big toe on each foot that works like a thumb.

2. Orangutans are the only kind of **ape** found in Asia.

3. Unlike other apes, orangutans prefer to live alone rather than in groups.

4. Orangutans eat mostly fruit.

5. There are two kinds of orangutans—Sumatran and Bornean. Both are **endangered**.

# Glossary

**ape** (APE) a large animal related to monkeys and humans

**endangered** (en-DAYN-jurd) in danger of dying out because of human activity

**shaggy** (SHAG-ee) rough, long, messy

**tropical** (TRAH-pih-kuhl) hot, rainy places on Earth

# Index